T. a. Ric

Oct. 1914

THE GERMAN EMPIRE'S HOUR
OF DESTINY

THE
GERMAN EMPIRE'S
HOUR OF DESTINY

BY

COLONEL H. FROBENIUS

With a Preface by
SIR VALENTINE CHIROL

AUTHOR OF "TWIXT GREEK AND TURK," "THE FAR EASTERN QUESTION," "THE MIDDLE EASTERN QUESTION," "INDIAN UNREST," ETC.

London
John Long, Limited
Norris Street, Haymarket
1914

TRANSLATED BY W. H. B.

PREFACE

SOME student of the historical phenomena of our times will doubtless one day work out a complete record of the warnings of the coming storm we have had out of the mouths of Germans themselves since Treitschke, the apocalyptic precursor of the Mailed Fist, first proclaimed that Germany must square accounts first with France and Russia and then proceed to the squaring of the last and greatest of her accounts—with England. When that record has been compiled, we shall hardly be able to charge the Germans with having sought to take us unawares. There are none so deaf as those who have not ears to listen, or who listen only to the things they like to hear. With the latter, indeed, our ears were plied to satiety through all the many official and unofficial channels which Germany had at her command, from the Emperor and his Ministers down to the personally conducted parties of amiable Teutons who periodically came over here with hatred in their hearts but with a keen eye to business and always with their pockets bulging out with messages of peace and goodwill. Only a nation as addicted as ourselves to contemptuous indifference in regard to all foreign countries could have failed to be struck with the contrast between the smooth language used before the footlights under the audible prompting of the Imperial stage manager, and what was being not merely said but done behind the scenes by the blood and iron authors of the new Teutonic drama: "World Empire or Downfall." Our prosperity had satisfied us that peace was the greatest of British interests, and, that being so, we hugged ourselves with the comfortable assumption that nobody else would try to disturb it. If peace was good enough for Englishmen, it was good enough for the rest of the world. That in Germany there was growing up a powerful school of thought which looked upon war as in itself a far higher thing than peace, and war with England, especially, as indispensable to the working out of Germany's destinies, was to most Englishmen incredible, as most things seem to be that lie entirely outside the range of one's own experience. When Germany, time and again, rejected with scorn and derision the proposals of the British Government to reduce the burden of armaments by common agreement, or to expand the area of international arbitration, or to mitigate the horrors of warfare by the solemn enactment of specific regulations, we spoke with sorrow rather than with indignation of her short-sightedness and comforted ourselves with the assurance that, in the long run, the forces of progress and peace must prevail in Germany, as everywhere else, over the mediæval influences of a German bureaucracy still imbued with some of the worst Bismarckian traditions. The few Englishmen who, having enjoyed better opportunities, had for many years past read the signs of the times in Germany, who had realized that a new generation was growing up which regarded even the Bismarckian traditions as too mild and cramped to achieve the boundless expansion of the Teutonic world empire, who had recognized that the German sword was no longer, as in Bismarck's days, merely the powerful weapon which German diplomacy controlled, but itself now controlled German diplomacy, did their best to enlighten their fellow-countrymen, but they were merely jeered at for their pains as mischievous alarmists who mistook the ravings of a few German fire-eaters for the voice of the great peace-loving German people. Some of our rulers, with the fuller knowledge they were bound to possess, saw, if only as through a glass darkly, the breakers ahead. But they hesitated to take the country into their complete confidence, and the measures they were from time to time compelled to take in order to secure a modicum of national safety were therefore too often only half measures brought forward with an apologetic half-heartedness which failed to carry conviction either to friends or to foes.

This translation of Colonel Frobenius's book, with the high-sounding title of *The German Empire's Hour of Destiny*, is the latest addition to the evidence with which, since the war broke out, the British public is being confronted of its blindness for so many years past to the true inwardness of German ambitions. He too is one of those who foreshadowed Germany's Next War, and though he is not possessed of the fine frenzy which inspires General von Bernhardi's works, and indeed looks mainly to an American, General Homer Lea, for his text, his businesslike discussion of the military problem to which Germany would have to

address herself, is none the less valuable.
As for all the writers of this school, England
is for him the enemy *par excellence*. But in
some respects he surpasses them all by im-
puting to her, even in the conduct of the
coming war, the same Machiavellian du-
plicity which has, of course, in his opinion
characterized her diplomatic preparations
for it. " The world is governed only by
trickery and deceit," wrote Frederick the
Great to Voltaire, and the Emperor William
prides himself, above all, on being the direct
heir of the Frederickian tradition. But he
who puts his faith in trickery and deceit and
makes a constant practice of them, is apt to
assume that everyone else does the same, and
this assumption lands him in grievous mis-
calculations. Colonel Frobenius has stum-
bled badly into this very pitfall. He believes,
of course, in the first place that England,
whilst anxious to see Germany involved in a
life and death struggle with France and
Russia, would do her best to keep out of the

conflict herself, with a view to profiting, as she has always done, by the ultimate exhaustion of the belligerent Powers. But should she come in, it would be only for the purpose of destroying the German Navy, of which she has watched the growth with jealous alarm; even if her military resources allowed her to take any part in the hostilities on land, it would not be in her interest and therefore she would not care to assist the French Army which, if victorious over Germany, would in its turn become once more, as it has been in the past, a source of disquietude to the British Islands. Colonel Frobenius, it should be added, is good enough to impute equally mean *arrière pensées* to our allies. France and Russia, according to him, would like to destroy the German Army, but they would also like to preserve the German Navy as a counter to be subsequently employed against the increasing predominance of England. It is a singular and also a reassuring feature in the disquisitions of all these apostles of brute force that, however sound their military theories may prove to have been, their political calculations have, for the most part, already hopelessly miscarried. The reason is not far to seek. Their military theories dealt with forces which are capable of more or less exact calculation; their political estimates ignored all those moral *imponderabilia* of which Bismarck himself was fain to recognize the immense importance. No doubt, in a world ruled wholly by brute force, as the world would be if they had their way, they would be right, for all moral forces, ponderable or imponderable, would have ceased to exist. But happily, though Colonel Frobenius has been specially blessed by no less exalted a personage than the Crown Prince of Germany himself, that time is not yet.

Valentine Chirol.

CONTENTS

The German Empire's Hour of Destiny

It cannot be maintained that the unification of the German races and the reconstitution of the German Empire in 1870-1871 awakened much pleasure in any European State. To the Powers the balance of Europe seemed upset, as a Power worthy of respect arose in the central territory which had furnished them with a welcome battle-ground, and the small states had great fear of " rapacious and land greedy Germany " which the experience of forty-three years of peace has not yet mitigated. And yet this new strong military Empire has proved itself by its restraint, even to the sacrifice of its just claims, the mighty shield to which we are principally indebted for this long period of peace.

During this time there has been no lack of occasions, and it has often required the high statecraft of a Bismarck to promptly extinguish the glowing sparks which threatened to set fire to all Europe; but since Russia is no longer bound by any treaty, since her interests have thrown her into the arms of France, and since England has considered her economic and military dominion of the world threatened by Germany, unfavourable circumstances are beginning to shape themselves against the German Empire, so that it will not much longer be able to patiently bear the burden and we shall probably have to reckon in the not distant future with a solution by recourse to arms. Let us consider what interests the principal, and therefore the most dangerous, opponents would really have in such a war which will undoubtedly involve the whole of Europe.

I

GREAT BRITAIN

AN American, but at the same time a
keen Anglo-Saxon, Homer Lea, recently
published a book, *The Day of the Saxon*,
which has been translated by Count E. Revent-
low under the title of *Des Britischen Reiches
Schicksalstunde* (Berlin, 1913 ; E. S. Mittler
and Sohn), in which he pictures the dangers
which threaten the British world empire, in-
asmuch as England has lost so much of her
fitness for war and has so neglected her war
preparations, especially with regard to the
maintenance of a sufficient army on land,
that she is no longer in a position to protect
her colossal possessions. " The old ideals

which produced the world empire have been laid aside. The warlike spirit is only of secondary consideration : it is hardly anything further than that spirit of commerce, slothful and satiated with the accumulation of things which are useless for national and racial progress."

On the other hand this world empire, which extends over and controls all available corners of the earth, presents grave difficulties to the expansion of other nations, so that a conflict with those States which chiefly require expansion, namely, Germany and Japan, is unavoidable because assured communication with the oceans of the world, which is vital to their interests, furnishes the motive for such expansion, whereas, on the other hand, Russia still has vast territories at the disposal of her rapidly increasing population. Homer Lea considers Germany the most dangerous opponent of the British world empire, and in his view England should never have permitted the unification thereof.

England should rather have utilized the disintegration and dismemberment of post-Napoleonic Europe in order to make herself over-lord of that Continent. Whether England had the opportunity and capacity to do this the author does not attempt to consider.

As a matter of fact, Germany has since 1870 become a dangerous, not opponent, but competitor of Great Britain in the world's markets. The first breach in the highly developed industry of Great Britain was made by Alfred Krupp as long ago as 1851 when he exhibited at the London Exhibition against the best effort of English steel works, namely, a block of 1,000 lbs., a similar block of 2,000 kilogrammes in weight; and, as he was able at the World's Exhibition of 1862 to exhibit breech-loading guns and great shafts for vessels together with a block of forty thousand pounds in weight, he for all time captured for the German iron trade the premier position which had so long been stubbornly held by England. The proved perfection of his drawn steel guns in the war of 1870-71 assured German gun manufacturers a position all over the world which, thanks to the untiring energy of our manufacturers, could not be shaken by the greatest efforts of English industry. Into the breach opened by Krupp aspiring representatives of other industries courageously sprang and the trade which developed hand in hand with them to all corners of the earth soon enabled Germany to become an important rival in the markets of the world.

But not yet a dangerous one, because as long as the British Fleet had the mastery of all means of communication at sea all the splendour of the German Commercial Marine could be easily swept away at the first opportunity. The commercial war only became dangerous when Germany commenced to build war vessels for protection of her commerce, and eventually changed her ideas from what was originally intended to be only a coast defence force to a battle fleet which became a considerable factor of German war power. The political grounds for England's opposition, therefore, primarily rest on an astonishing but frequently reappearing fear of our sea power. In order to obtain a clear view of the motives hitherto underlying her policy we will examine England's past history.

Since that country has played a part in the history of sea Powers, that is to say since she determined to obtain for herself a position on the sea, her opponent has always from time to time been the strongest sea Power. Thus, just as she was the constant enemy of the world Powers Spain and Portugal so long as they ruled on the sea, England turned against Holland as soon as the latter, after her release from the Spanish yoke, had won her dominion on the sea. And as soon as the latter, in unfortunate misapprehension of her real requirements and hard pressed on her frontiers, neglected her navy, England immediately took up her attitude against another Power, France, which strengthened itself at sea under the wise guidance of Colbert. This enmity England maintained so long as no other Power became more dangerous. On every occasion when France, driven by her restless ambitious policy, was involved in a conflict, we find England on the side of her opponents and also even when English interests were not directly in question. And we find this continuing until some other Power appeared which could threaten the Island realm more directly than our western neighbour.

Slowly but uninterruptedly Russia had extended its borders in Asia; with exceptional stubbornness had pushed its Cossack hordes towards the east and south, and England saw that she had to make immediate preparations, as her own efforts to expand from the direction of India would knock up against Russian opposition. The dangerous situation was that in that direction her strength left something to be desired, that is to say she might easily come off second best in a conflict in the interior of Asia. So an opportunity had to be found by which this future enemy could be combated at sea. This was found when Russia attempted, in the Turkish War, to increase her power in the Balkans. The Crimean war broke out and we suddenly find England as companion in arms of her former hereditary enemy France, against the new and dangerous opponent. For some time peace seemed to reign between the two sea Powers ; but this state of affairs did not last long. Even if since that date they have not actually come to blows it may well be remembered what embittered diplomatic struggles the partition of Africa and France's renewed colonial expansion in Asia and the Mediterranean in the last quarter of the past century led to between the two Powers. In 1889 England effected a powerful increase of her fleet as against France's sea power, and in 1898 both fleets were actually mobilized in consequence of the Fashoda dispute. Then came the first German Navy law.

At one stroke England's policy changed its front. Whereas up to that time the development of Germany's marine interests had not been regarded from the English point of view with very kindly feelings and attempts had been made, where possible, to hinder them, from that moment a diplomatic war set in against us which we have since been accustomed to regard as permanent. We should not be deceived by a temporary apparently friendly disposition; this generally conceals secret feelings of malevolence. And the whole course of past British history confirms this. As soon as our vigorous determined German people, under the rule of a far seeing sovereign, resolved to create a weapon which could be utilized on the sea, then according to English principles such must always be fought, as the most dangerous—the enemy. But it must be understood that he is the enemy because he is building a fleet; when this has been destroyed then at one blow all cause of enmity will have disappeared. With the fleet destroyed it may be concluded that German commerce would be robbed of its absolutely necessary protection and after destruction of its mercantile marine it would withdraw from the world's markets in a condition of impotence from which it would only be in a position to recover slowly and with great exertions.

Homer Lea is, however, of opinion that the British World Empire can only be saved by the complete ruin of Germany and the military relations of the two present to him a double aspect; " The Anglo-Saxon can only fight Russia on land, Japan only on the water; a war with Germany involves a fight on land and water. The difficulties of this contest will demand the full means and powers of those concerned; they will be twice as great as in an Anglo-Russian contest or Anglo-Japanese contest." . . . If the British Navy destroys the German Fleet the only result will be the same position as before the war, but at any rate the United Kingdom will no longer have to apprehend immediate danger. But even such a victory would not bring England nearer to the destruction of the power of Germany and her possibilities of a world-wide expansion than was the case before the war, " for only in the case of a war between Great Britain and another Island nation would the navy be of paramount importance. In a war with Russia the navy would have no place at all. In a war of aggression against Germany it would be of secondary importance. The British Navy has one sole mission ; to remain mistress of the sea. From beginning to end it is directed to defence. The army alone possesses the capacity and power of deciding a war and bringing about such a peace as will prolong the existence of the World Empire." He emphasizes the fact that it is essential for the future greatness of Germany to destroy the Anglo-Saxon World-dominion and to build up its own World power out of the ruins, and he explains that it is for that reason it is the first duty of England to destroy the German forces.

On such grounds Homer Lea founds Great Britain's need to create an army which will be superior in any war on land by adoption of universal military service not only in her Island kingdom but also in her colonies. Many efforts have been made in this direction in England, especially in recent times and with the support of moderate persons, without succeeding in overcoming the opposition of the nation. Such a measure would not only cut into the deep rooted ideas of personal freedom, but would also be contrary to England's custom (which has always been skilfully and happily preserved) of exploiting on land the military powers of other nations and extracting from their loss of blood the double advantage of overcoming unpleasant resistance to herself and bringing about a wholesome weakening of her allies. For possibly within a short time the latter might develop into an enemy who would have to be fought. And might not such a custom be considered appropriate as regards Germany?

But as to this anon. Let us first give a hurried glance at the measures of Britain for securing her permanent over-lordship of the ocean, which are not only adapted to the Island Empire's commerce but also to her readiness for war. With wonderful acuteness she has ever been successful in finding and, regardless of others, annexing in all parts of the ocean such spots as control the important routes. By means of Gibraltar the entrance to the Mediterranean is closed, through Malta the connection between its western and eastern basins, and through Cyprus she has assured the entrance to the Suez Canal, which with Egypt is absolutely hers. By that means she controls the shortest water-way to India, the Indian Ocean and the Pacific. But she is also in a position to exercise her influence over the longer route round

Africa by means of St. Helena and Ascension as well as her African colonies, whilst the outlet from the Red Sea to the Straits of Bab-el-Mandeb is closed by the Island of Perim. The road to the Pacific proceeds further through the Straits of Malacca, and at this spot a British Naval Harbour was recently built at Singapore. It should be possible for the European States by construction of railways to free themselves of England's lordship of the water routes, and Russia succeeded in establishing a connection with the Pacific by means of the Siberian Railway, but the desire, thereby to obtain a constantly open harbour, was frustrated with the help of Japan. Germany commenced the construction of the Anatolian and Bagdad Railway; but soon thereafter England succeeded in wresting from Turkey the important terminus Koweit and so multiplied the obstacles which she was already in a position to impose to the outlet from the Persian Gulf by possession of the Island of Bahrain and the

29

Ras Dschask. Only one sea-route—a recently created one—has been withdrawn from British influence : the Panama Canal which connects the Caribbean Sea or, as it may be called, the American Mediterranean, direct with the Pacific, and thereby Great Britain's absolute command of the sea has, it must be confessed, suffered a serious blow.

The Island Empire will have to tolerate the participation of other nations with strong navies—and in the first place in the Pacific— but this only with the neighbouring states of Japan and North America who possess defensive positions in that ocean, and perhaps with France who would like to save the remains of her over-sea possessions in India from the covetousness of England and to further extend her dominion in Madagascar and further India. Not with Germany, which throughout the whole distance of its possessions in Africa to the Pacific does not possess a single place of shelter.

And it is not only free water ways which

navigation requires, since sailing ships have been completely replaced in the navy and largely in the mercantile marine by steamships. As all human progress can only be won by sacrifice, navigation has had to surrender its unlimited freedom of action as against the great advantages of steam : it is absolutely dependent on supplies of fuel for its boilers. But as a warship has to carry considerable loads in the shape of armour, guns and ammunition, even the largest battleships cannot exceed a certain load of fuel and to that extent the duration and length of the voyage, with supplies sufficient to maintain a certain rate of speed without re-coaling, are limited ; that is to say, the useful activity of the ship suffers. Therefore if supplies cannot be renewed the ship is just as incapable of continuing her voyage as a locomotive, which has run out of coals and water.

With the introduction of steamships all seafaring nations were therefore obliged to take into consideration the acquisition of coaling stations at certain intervals, for which purpose of course only islands or places on the coast were suitable which presented ample protection for shipment of coal and to which end it was necessary to acquire the proprietorship. And at this point Great Britain proceeded to acquire for herself not only an efficient medium in her commercial competition with Germany but also in case of need a considerable obstacle to the employment of Germany's navy in war time. She was clever enough to be able to frustrate every attempt of the German Empire to acquire points of support or at any rate coaling stations on the coasts of the seas of the world. All movements and enterprises of German ships were followed with suspicious eyes so as immediately and actively to oppose by diplomatic means or even by direct threats all attempts to acquire any spot adaptable as a coal base even if such intention were only remotely suspected. Everyone will remember that in the dispute over Morocco France showed herself quite willing to hand over to Germany certain territory, but England's threatening attitude stiffened her back and compelled us to give up all claim to any Moroccan possession. In consequence of this attitude of our cousins across the Channel, Germany's mercantile marine and navy are obliged to rely for their coal supplies on the depots of other nations and principally of England. In addition to the fact that our ships have to pay the prices asked for this hospitality and the advantage goes to the foreigner, it becomes a serious question where we are to find anywhere on the globe, friendly nations who will be able to provide our ships with fuel in time of war. The harbours of England and France will assuredly be closed to us, and it is more than doubtful whether the Colonies of small European States would, in face of Great Britain's threats, dare to remain open to us. Here we have a very substantial instance where we require freedom of action and where England has fettered our requirements for expansion; in this direction it is necessary for us sooner or later to break these chains which are, if maintained, intolerable to our navigation, and must in case of war constitute a grave danger. But to this end it is not necessary to destroy the Anglo-Saxon World dominion which Homer Lea declares to be absolutely necessary for the future greatness of Germany. Germany's wants could be easily satisfied out of the excessive abundance of England's possessions. But it seems as if England desires to continue the contest for sole command of the sea. And therefore it must be her principle always to fight the State that may become the most dangerous, and first of all Japan before the latter grows into too powerful an opponent in the Pacific. But for such purpose she would require all her maritime forces and this may appear to her a doubtful enterprise in face of the strong German Navy. For that reason she favours the course of using the first favourable opportunity of destroying the latter, her present opponent, and thus winning full freedom of action in the Pacific. But for this object the destruction of the German Fleet would be sufficient and it would not require the complete destruction of the German Empire, which Homer Lea considers necessary.

Great Britain has acquired another arm through her network of cables by which she has bound together all parts of the world with the Island Kingdom. A rapid means of communication of news is of exceptional importance for commerce as well as for naval warfare. It enables a concentration of management which can take advantage of every favourable situation and which is in a position to avoid every threatening danger and to spring on the enemy, who is excluded from this news service, the most unpleasant surprises. So long as England was the sole mistress of the whole cable service she could at will close its use to other nations and impose complete deafness and blindness on them with regard to events in distant spots, keeping for herself alone means of sight and hearing and so secure to herself all the advantages of initiative. The acknowledgment of this danger has not so long back induced other nations to lay cables which are capable of communicating news across the sea independently of the English connections, at any rate in respect of some zones. But in the first place this is not a complete network, and secondly there is some danger that in case of war Great Britain might cut the cables which are not under her control and render them useless.

The invention of wireless telegraphy now provides a means of release from cable connections. England therefore followed the further development of this science with great attention and was successful in procuring the establishment of the Marconi Company in England. She made the greatest efforts to secure the monopoly of wireless telegraphy and therefore to rule the world by this means of communication. Thanks to German science this did not succeed. We have surpassed the efficiency of Marconi's apparatus and by that means have won for ourselves certain compensation for the network of cables which we do not possess. True, up to now only within certain limits, that is to say, in so far as our apparatus are able to work efficiently and in so far as we possess stations which can pass on news. It is therefore of the greatest importance that the Emperor was recently able to exchange a wireless conversation with the President of the United States of America by means of our apparatus. It is quite comprehensible and universally acknowledged that England by way of precautionary measures against a serious conflict with Germany has secured powerful allies. It is not yet quite clear to what extent, in addition to Russia and France, smaller States such as Belgium, Denmark, the Balkan States, etc., are concerned. As they will have to reckon not only with the German

Empire but also with the members of the Triple Alliance, it has become apparent that the parts which the three Powers will play have been distributed. Great Britain herself is acknowledgedly working to conceal her objects and to lull to sleep the German Michael, but on the other hand presents a stern countenance to Italy. The latter's growing fleet and especially the possession of the Turkish islands in the Ægean Sea, which have remained in her possession since the Turco-Italian War, constitute a very uncomfortable factor for the complete command of the Mediterranean. It even appears that the Porte is quite satisfied and therefore delays the withdrawal of the last of her officers from the Tripoli Hinterland, as meanwhile Italy is justified in retaining the Islands, a circumstance which ensures them against attempts by others to secure them. Now, as Sir Edward Grey has expressed the opinion that the situation in Europe will not become normal so long as a great Power possesses these Islands, it is easy to see how uneasily Italy regards the pressure which the English Minister desires to exercise. And the more so as at the same time he was desirous of leaving the evacuation of the part of Albania, which was still in the possession of the Greeks, entirely in their discretion, and they in raising " Holy Battalions " in the territory in question do not present a very complaisant attitude. I should put against Homer Lea's proposition, that Great Britain to maintain her position as a World Power must annihilate Germany—that is to say not only rob her of her fleet and cripple her commerce but also destroy her land forces—the view that England can have no desire to annihilate our army. That would be contrary to the whole of her policy to date. A strong Power on land on the European Continent is indispensable to her so that she may induce it to go to war on land against any State which might become dangerous to her sea power. This is the principle on which she has always played the political game with the Powers on the mainland. For example, at the commencement of the Austrian War of Succession France was England's most dangerous rival on the seas, as she was considerably increasing her Colonial possessions. Austria was the great Power on land, and therefore the Island Kingdom lent her support in the struggle against Prussia who was allied with France. After she had commenced in 1755 to come into direct conflict with France at sea she had to forego assistance to Austria, who had become allied with Russia and France to overcome Frederick the Great, and placed herself on the side of the King of Prussia whom she had recently been fighting. But when she had attained her object, when in 1758 she had driven the French ships from the East Indies and taken the French possessions in Senegal, when in 1760 by the capture of Montreal she had torn Canada from the French and had put to shame their navy that she could put her full power in the West

Indies and limit herself in European waters to a blockade, when therefore the soaring power of France had been utterly destroyed in all quarters of the globe, she quite unexpectedly withdrew her support from the Prussian Alliance. Prussia had done her duty in leading off French activity from the sea. She could now look after herself in dealing with her enemy, as England had no further cause for damaging the latter. This sudden change of front is usually associated with the resignation of Pitt, as if the latter's friendship with Frederick had determined the attitude of Great Britain. But such sentimental feelings cannot be credited to an English Statesman.

Austria is no longer capable of continuing to play the part against France which England formerly assigned to her. On the other hand a new Power has arisen in Russia, whose vital interests are in direct conflict with those of England. The equilibrium can only be maintained as regards Russia if a strong military force can be put up against her. France is not suitable for this purpose, as after the prostration of Germany the former would immediately re-enter the lists as the second European sea and Colonial Power against England. This rôle against Russia can therefore only be assigned to Germany; and the alliance of England and Russia against Germany which is obviously contrary to the interests of both sides, in addition to the fervent wish to break the latter's commercial power, is also—perhaps only unconsciously—invested with the object of thoroughly undermining the old friendship of both States, in order to play off the German against the Russian at some future date. Therefore England has no object in annihilating Germany's land forces—on the contrary her object in war can only be the destruction of the latter's Navy, sparing if possible her Army.

The question comes whether the superior English battle fleet is alone capable of doing this. This question is answered by a British author, J. S. Corbett, an acknowledged expert and lecturer on Naval Strategy, who has laid down universally accepted principles in his work *Some Principles of Maritime Strategy*, and relies on the methods of conducting a Naval War which have hitherto prevailed. According to him the whole history of naval warfare shows that a fight between two fleets directed to the destruction of one of them can only take place with the consent of both parties. The desire of both sides not to avoid a decisive action can alone bring about such a result in open battle ; but this can only be presumed if each side considers it has a chance of success, that is to say, if they are approximately equal in strength. If this be not so, the weaker side will according to experience diligently endeavour to draw the other on and so to gradually weaken him by small attacks and diminish his powers that a grand assault may eventually be risked with chances of success. In the face of such tactics the stronger side, as Corbett maintains, has always found itself in a difficult position. Every day by which a decision is postponed wastes much money—and nowadays coal in addition, which it is always difficult to replace. Every day may bring unpleasant surprises, and therefore he must try and bring about a decisive result as quickly as possible. To this end only two ways are open; he must either attempt to destroy by force under fire of coast defences the obstructions by means of which the enemy has secured himself in his hiding place, and force an entrance into the harbour into which the latter has retired—(and he has rarely possessed the courage for that)—or he must attempt to bombard him out. This is however not usually possible from seawards in the case of well designed war harbours, but only through forces which have been landed for this purpose and which have been provided with the necessary heavy artillery so as to win by quick assault positions which will enable the shelling of the enemy's fleet anchored in harbour, and compel it to come out and seek battle. Examples of this are furnished by the tactics of the Americans at San Jago de Cuba and the Japanese at Port Arthur. The question arises whether in the coming war with Germany the Continental Powers for the time being allied with Great Britain will perform this duty, and this cannot be affirmed with certainty because the interests clash. Both Powers seek a decision by the nearest road between Berlin and their Capitals and have no inducement to divide and weaken their forces by devoting not inconsiderable masses of troops and heavy material to the investment of our marine fortresses. They would much rather destroy Germany's land forces but if possible spare her navy as a menace to their future enemy Great Britain. They will be just as much alive as we are to the hitherto constant policy of England, and to foresee such future hostility. Therefore if England wishes to attain her object in war, the destruction of the German Navy, she will *nolens volens* have to devote her own forces thereto and we shall not be far wrong in assuming that the British expeditionary force of 150,000 men will be destined as an invading force to support her fleet.

The further question, how this invading force is to be handled, especially to what extent it is to take part in the operations of the allied land forces and to be treated as reinforcements thereof may likewise be answered by some words of the English naval strategist. They are as follows :—

"This is certain, whoever commands the sea possesses full freedom of trade and can derive as much or as little profit from the war as he pleases, whilst even the strongest land force will experience great difficulties." (Page 55.)

"If the scope of the war was unlimited, and in consequence thereof the whole power of the enemy is called out on that principle, it is clear that a decisive result could only be obtained after his forces have been completely shattered. If it was not the intention to attempt this then it was false policy to endeavour to reach the goal by force, that is to say the war should not have been entered into. In the case of a limited object the annihilation of the whole of the enemy's defences is outside the scope of what was necessary." (Page 42.)

" If we now turn to England's experience in Continental wars we find that she often took part in a war on land, and we also find that she almost, without exception, ran up against the great reluctance of the people, as if there were something in it repugnant to national instincts." (Page 60.)

These three quotations give us a complete picture of England's customary manner of taking part in the wars of Continental Powers. Since the commencement of the seventeenth century she always had at her disposal the necessary means of assuring

D   47

herself of the command of the sea, or at any rate of maintaining a very favourable situation, which Corbett calls " combative command of the sea." This fortunate country was almost invariably in the position of interfering in the wars of European Powers and " getting for herself as much as she wanted."

What she did want, we see from the second quotation. Corbett is an admirer of our strategist Clausewitz, and follows that teacher in discriminating between the two different kinds of war, the limited and unlimited. Clausewitz describes it in the words : " This two-fold method of war consists of, (1) where the object is the prostration of the enemy, either annihilating him politically or simply disarming him and therefore forcing him to the desired conditions of peace, and (2) where it is simply desired to wrest from him certain possessions on the frontiers of his Kingdom either for the purpose of keeping them permanently or using them as a useful means of exchange on the declaration of peace."

48

The first case demands the entire exertions of the whole people, the second does not. Clausewitz gives an illuminating example of war with limited objects in a Memorandum of 1830-31 which contains a project of a war against France. Circumstances did not permit the taking into consideration of the complete prostration of that State, and the programme of our strategists was therefore directed to making the annexation of Belgium the real object of the attack.

" This country of moderate size and great resources is surrounded by Holland and Germany ; consequently after its annexation the army of occupation will not find itself at the corner of a triangle extending into a large hostile territory, and for that reason such an annexation could be permanently maintained under ordinary circumstances. . . . However strongly the French may establish themselves in Belgium they would still, as they are situated, be weaker there than in the middle of their own country.

When the command of the Meuse has been obtained the annexation of Belgium may be regarded as an actual fact. . . . We therefore consider that if the allied forces can gain a victory anywhere (and this must be considered as necessary ' in every offensive design '), such victory would produce the easiest yet least secure result in the annexation of Belgium."

If we examine the history of England we must acknowledge that she at times exerted herself to the uttermost by the utilization of individual portions of her armament, navy, and finances, but never has known that demand on the whole of her population by calling out every man capable of bearing arms as Prussia and Germany did in 1813 and France in 1870. She was careful to avoid this by never having in view unlimited aims, which is a brilliant illustration of Clausewitz's precepts. She never, with the exception of her colonial wars, desired to completely annex any country, or completely annihilate any enemy. The objects which she desired to attain by her own powers were also limited; with the exception of certain over-sea possessions, the destruction of hostile marine forces or commercial interests. This may have arisen partly from a very clever policy and partly also may have had its reason in the sentiments of the people, as mentioned by Corbett. The English people never had any feeling or sympathy for the exacting military service necessary for wars on land, which presses the rifle into the hands of the masses and tears them from their hearths and homes. She either employed mercenaries for this purpose or knew how to make her allies bleed for her, and as far as the latter were concerned the war easily became an unlimited one. In this respect we need only refer again to the wars of Frederick the Great.

Therefore, England only wages wars of limited scope and employs her army unwillingly. From this point of view one may draw conclusions as to her future conduct with regard to the employment of her army of invasion as to which Corbett again gives an indication. He says :—

" The expeditionary force must either unreservedly take part as an organic unit of the Power which is conducting the unlimited war, or a certain territorial area of operations must be assigned to it with independent leadership and with an organization independent of the Commander-in-Chief of the allied force, but with limited activity." (Page 59.)

" But that which may be called the British or maritime method is in fact the application of limited methods in the conduct of an unlimited war in combination with the larger operations of our allies—a method which has generally been open to us as it has enabled our command of the sea to select a theatre of war which was in fact limited." (Page 63.)

This illustrates the whole peculiarity of England's conduct of wars on land. They presume that their continental ally will have to conduct an unlimited war, as the chief burden will be gradually put on to him. It is on the other hand emphasized as typically British that the expeditionary force must, if possible, be kept away from the latter plan. Its co-operation, therefore, as an organic portion of our enemy's forces is only to be looked for if Great Britain actually has no other means of reaching her special goal.

But the clearest explanation of all is afforded by a glance at military history, as Corbett explains it.

Since the war of the Spanish succession, in which Marlborough with the British auxiliary forces marched deep into the South of Germany in order to fight in combination with the Imperial troops sanguinary and decisive battles against Louis XIV, an English force has never again wandered about on the Continent whenever the slightest uncertainty was present. Particularly in Holland, and in the wars of Frederick the Great in Hanover, that is to say, always close to the sea coast, we see British troops carrying on a slow and laborious war and carefully avoiding a decisive result. Who will forget the feeble behaviour of the Duke of Cumberland, of which Fontenoy in 1745, Lafeld in 1747, Hastenbeck in 1757, and the capitulation at Kloster Zeven are examples?

Likewise in the course of the Spanish War against Napoleon, in which the unlucky Moore was replaced by the more skilful Lord Wellesley, we see, so long as the enemy was not rendered completely powerless, a careful maintenance of communication with the sea. And wherever such was interrupted on one side it was at once skilfully reunited in another direction. On one occasion only do we see an English force taking part in a decisive battle, at Waterloo. But on this occasion hesitation to obtain a decisive result presented the danger of a very undesirable prolongation of the war in case of defeat of the allied continental forces, and

Wellington found himself in a peculiar difficulty.

" Therefore, all through we see the endeavour to keep up communication with the base, that is to say, for England, with the sea coast, in so far as practicable harbours are available for embarkation, and to avoid every decisive action so long as this is not enforced by the situation ; and at the same time to avoid too close a junction with the operations of the allies : that is what may be called the British or maritime method."

With these premises we may now endeavour to picture to ourselves the probable procedure of Great Britain in case of a conflict with Germany.

She would, of course, most of all desire entirely independent action for her land forces, and if she is assured, through the preparations and available numbers of her allies' forces, that the latter will be able to deal alone with our armies, she will be able to preserve for herself this independence through being able to choose the theatre of her operations. If she cannot be certain of this, and if the independent action of her expeditionary force becomes doubtful, then she will have to take part as an organic unit in the larger operations. In that case a landing in Belgium, previously entirely freed from the influence of German troops, would enable the British troops to furnish an extension of the French left wing.

We are involuntarily reminded of the opposition which was raised in the English Press to Holland's scheme of renewing the old fortifications of Flushing, and replacing them with new constructions, which would not only protect the recently enlarged harbour against an enemy but would also prove an obstacle to the navigation of the West Scheld to Antwerp.

In view of the indisputable right of the sovereign state to provide an important harbour for the protection of its fleet (Holland only possesses one other, namely, the Helder), and to fulfil the duties imposed upon it by its neutrality, it strikes one as peculiar that the Press of France and Belgium, in combination with the English Press, endeavoured by ingenious and untenable arguments and representations to intimidate the Dutch into wrecking the plans of the Government.

Therefrom must be drawn the evidence for the assumption that England, in case of a conflict with Germany, intends to land her expeditionary force in Antwerp so as to support France. And even if the new fortifications of Flushing, whilst limited to a single fort on the right bank, may not be capable of holding out any length of time against an assault, yet they might exert a very disturbing influence on the entrance of such a large fleet of transports as would be required for the passage of the British Army, and would very much delay an intended landing at Antwerp. Everything would depend upon the great speed of this movement. Otherwise British assistance would come too late and would be practically valueless.

Let us assume that the British expeditionary force would by this means, or some other, join the French left wing and take a timely part in the operations; and if we assume that the first great success will have been obtained over our army and that the latter has its hands full with the French forces, then the curtain will draw up on the second act of the operations of the British troops, as they will then be able to free themselves from the undesirable "unlimited" method and be able to proceed independently, that is to say, they will seek "a limited area of operation." According to Great Britain's War Game this can only be the German North Sea coast, to the harbours of which the German fleet, as being the weaker, will in our view have retired. The British Navy will be ready lying in wait for the German ships which will be driven out by the artillery of the land forces attacking the fortresses, and will be ready to destroy it, as was done at Port Arthur.

What period of time this would demand it is impossible to judge. The experience of Port Arthur warns us that it would involve heavy sacrifices both of time and lives. At any rate, the goal cannot be reached in a turn of the hand; and, therefore, it is not impossible that the investing army's lines of communication with French or Belgian harbours will be gravely endangered by German operations. England has always shown great skill in changing her lines of communication when these were in danger. A good example of her methods under such circumstances is furnished by England's Campaign in Spain against Napoleon in the years 1808 and 1809.

Napoleon advanced victoriously from Madrid against the British troops in Portugal. An English Corps under the command of Sir John Moore, which he believed to be in retreat, evaded him and threatened his lines

of communication from the direction of the
Douro. On Napoleon turning against him and
breaking his (Moore's) lines of communication
with Lisbon he withdrew to the north-west,
followed by the French Marshal, Soult, and
in the meantime the British General, Baird,
had landed at Corunna. Although the ships
were late, and Moore had to give battle in
front of the town, in which he himself fell,
the embarkation was successful and the
English Corps was enabled to return home.

In case of a war against Germany, England
has made ample preparations and has secured
herself a second line of communication, as
she has exercised great influence on the
enlargement of the hitherto very small
harbour of Esbjerg, on the Danish West
Coast of Jutland. Esbjerg is only about
twenty-eight kilometres from the Danish-
German Frontier, and possesses a bay including an outer, inner, boat, and fishing
harbour of about 15.7 hectares with 3.8 to
6 metres depth of water. The channel

through the Grautief has a uniform depth of over 7.5, but was closed by a sand bar, through which a passage was dredged.

These conditions were quite sufficient for the trade in butter and eggs carried in English ships. But now the harbour basins are being first extended to 40.50 hectares, and 2,800 metres of quay are being built, which enclose a harbour space capable of being dredged out to approximately 80 hectares, and the depth of water is to be brought up to eight metres. It is obvious that such a disproportionate extension of the harbour works cannot be attributed to the export of butter and eggs.

There can be no doubt that in case of a war Denmark will be found on the side of our enemies. That is evidenced by all the new defence works of that kingdom. The marine fortresses of Copenhagen are being increased and strengthened principally for closing the Channel (primarily the Drogden) in a southerly direction, thus towards

German waters. The land fortress which
would chiefly be employed against an attack
from the North is being neglected and will
probably be entirely abandoned. But still
more important are the new defences of the
Great Belt. Flanking this is a broad bay
between the Islands of Seeland, Falster,
Laaland and Langeland, the outlets of which
are all closed by forts, so that it resembles
a fox's earth. It offers innumerable hiding
places on the broken coasts of the Islands
which enable a sudden pounce not only on
the bay of Kiel and the Fehmarn Belt but
also on the outlet of Oere Sound, and is
extraordinarily difficult to attack. It was
quite superfluous for the Minister Neergard
to announce the object of this fortified bay
as follows : " The means of communication
by several routes with the theatre of war at
sea, thereby making it possible to attack
the enemy's fleet." So if, on the one hand,
Belgium is selected as a means to enable the British invading force to join in

a war with unlimited aims in its first proceeding, Denmark is given the part in the second proceeding, the war of limited scope, of (in our case) furnishing strong support in an assault on German harbours and the destruction of our fleet and providing a base for the employment of the land forces.*

With the exception of small unimportant operations of the British Navy, Great Britain would, according to Corbett, hand over to her allies the task of keeping the German land forces so employed that only weak detachments thereof could be sent to combat the English operations, whereas the latter's sole object would be the annihilation of our fleet, and for this purpose the landing force would only have to deal with inferior forces.

Now the question comes whether England's allies are quite agreeable to such a division

---

* It should be remembered that the nearest British harbour, Yarmouth, is nearly three and a half times as far from the mouth of the Elbe as Esbjerg, which therefore offers a favourable *point d'appui* to the English fleet.

of labour and the limitation of the British forces to this narrow sphere. According to the opinions of an anonymous French officer of the General Staff, this is very doubtful. He expresses himself on the principal points as follows* :—

1. Object of landing. "As far as the strategic point of view is concerned this will depend on the general military situation. It may be necessary to hasten to the assistance of the French against the German troops invading France, or to help the Russians, who may be pressed by the Germans and Austrians on the Weichsel and the Dniester." (Pages 32-33.)

"A feeling of uneasiness will be awakened ; the people will become unruly ; the soldiers perhaps defeated. . . . All that gradually creates a breach in the self-reliance of all concerned. . . . Other allies may appear on

* *Die Englische Invasion in Deutschland,* von einem französischen General-stabs-offizier. Published by *Politik,* Berlin, 1912.

the scene, Danes or Dutch according to circumstances. . . ." (Pages 7-8.)

2. Place of landing. In short—anywhere. The author favours the Ems and the mouth of the Weichsel; but he also considers other spots on the Baltic coast (Danish territory) suitable.

3. Method of landing. Deception as to the intended spot, and surprise.

Of course these opinions as to the employment of the British landing force are not to be regarded as applicable to the management of the French forces. At the same time they give an idea of the wishes entertained in general staff circles of our neighbour on the West and expressed to their British ally; they would like to consider the English expeditionary force as a purely auxiliary force, as reinforcements, not to operate independently according to a plan determined by the English Commander-in-Chief, but only placed ready to step in and help where the progress of war makes it desirable, and pull this or the other ally out of a difficulty, whether it be the French in their own country or the Russians on the Weichsel or Dniester. It is to be assumed that the English fleet will be able to deal with the German even without any support of land forces. The Allies do not trouble at all about the complete annihilation of the latter's fleet. This point of view cropped up on one occasion in connection with the pledge given by the English Government to France to send an auxiliary force in case of war with Germany. It was only conceived as being auxiliary to the French army, and there was no question of its independent employment for special purposes in England's interests. It seemed to be the opinion in France that Great Britain would quite unselfishly devote her forces to the interests of France. This is, of course, quite out of the question, as this State (England) has never subordinated her own interests to those of other states or nations, but on the contrary has, in many instances, made their forces serve her own ends and interests.

Therefore a great diversity of interests, evidenced by their divergent wishes, appears to arise between England and her allies; Great Britain desires to annihilate our navy whilst if possible sparing our army; France and Russia would like to destroy the German Army and preserve the Navy as a counter to be subsequently employed against the increasing predominance of England. It is interesting to observe from the opinions of the French officer that they confidently rely on the assistance of Denmark, and even of the Netherlands, but are discreetly silent about Belgium. If the co-operation of the neutral states is not opportunely secured before the commencement of the war it is to be attained by the appearance of English troops on the German coast, which may have a disastrous effect on the morale of our own troops, although, according to the author, the army of invasion on the coast would soon be stopped by the Germans and would then be relegated to the defensive. But it is not likely that England will agree to her landing force being paralysed in this manner.

The extraordinary preparations of both her allies were apparently designed to make England stiff-necked. If her design is to destroy the German Navy in any circumstances; if, according to Corbett's opinion, she is going to entrust to her expeditionary force a limited sphere of war and drive our fleet, if it withdraws into harbour, out under the fire of her battleships' guns, she cannot believe that the war will soon be terminated, as these operations will require time, much time.

But if superior French and Russian forces simultaneously invading Germany on both sides succeed (and this is what the abnormal preparations are for) in crushing our army by a few heavy blows, then England might not have sufficient time for her long-winded operations (investment of and capture of the harbours), and this is quite apart, as we just said, from the consideration that she has no interest in the complete destruction of the

German land forces. Perhaps that is why England is at present more amiably inclined towards us. Perhaps also the reflection is gaining ground that an attack on and destruction of our navy and commercial marine might not be carried out without sorrow and loss to her own country. Germany is Great Britain's best customer, and in many respects the latter relies on our industry. Great Britain has more trading ships on the sea than we have, and they are no less exposed to destruction by our cruisers than ours by the English.

Complete protection to English trading vessels on distant seas cannot be assured by their navy if they have to maintain in European waters the highest possible superiority over our fleet.

Finally, the Island Kingdom is to such a large extent dependent on the regular import of necessities of life, that a blockade would very quickly bring about a famine, coupled probably with very grave dangers. This is opportunely evidenced by the dockers' strike, which actually threatened the population of the capital with famine by depriving it of the imports which were in the docks. England has therefore to stomach these disadvantages against the advantages of her protected situation as regards invasion. So long as the Island Empire was actually mistress of the sea such conditions could not arise, and she could indulge in the luxury of neglecting her own agricultural production and devote all her energies to her industries, feeding herself from abroad. But those times are gone for ever. England cannot conceal from herself that she must even now share the command of the sea with other nations, and the destruction of our navy would not avail her, as navies are springing up in all directions and even wealthy Albion cannot continue to keep pace with the universal struggle for sea power. The less so as it is not only a question of the great expense but also in a very important degree of the manning of powerful battleships which are continually being added to and which are absolutely useless without very strong complements. We have lately been informed by Secretary of State von Tirpitz, that England's naval expenditure in the last five years has risen 216 millions but Germany's only 55 millions (marks or shillings); and that our expenditure is far less not only than England's but also than that of her two allies ; France's increase being 134, and Russia's for the Baltic fleet alone nearly 302 millions. That may cause Britain to think a bit. But with regard to the second point, the personnel, it is an open secret how difficult it is even on a moderate increase of a navy to provide in good time and train correspondingly increasing crews, and not only sailors but particularly engineers and officers. The difficulty which Great Britain in particular experiences in this respect is no secret. It is asserted—and it can hardly be a mistake—that Mr. Churchill suggested a year's holiday in naval construction to Germany in order to make up the deficiency in the personnel of the fleet. A crafty move, as England could amply employ her dockyards by building for other Powers, and would not even be obliged to go short, as in case of need she could impress into her own navy the foreign ships lying in her yards. But the stupid Michael did not enter the trap—simply because he did not know how otherwise to employ his dockyard hands during a whole year. The proposal, however, did contribute to make our Chamber of Deputies (Reichstag)—let us say—more careful—as the word "suspicious" is at present barred—in bewaring of our cousins on the other side of the Channel. And it will not be beside the purpose to remember that in 1870 England at the request of France made confidential inquiries of the Prussian Government whether the latter would not sanction a decrease in the Army, to be simultaneously effected by each State in the interests of the peace of Europe.

This happened almost immediately before the outbreak of war with France, on whose share in originating it I need not enlarge. (See Bismarck's letter of 9-2-1870.)

To be sure England has at present every reason for not seeking war with Germany without cause. It is said that the relations of the two States are happily developing on the lines of an understanding and *rapprochement* ; it is becoming acknowledged that they can work with and alongside each other on many points and questions, that their interests are identical in many respects. And as you call into a wood so a conciliatory echo replies. But it must not be forgotten that it was England that brought about this menacing coalition, which is at bottom unquestionably unnatural, because it has no common interests, and it was England that exerted herself to estrange us from our few remaining friends.

It can hardly be believed that our blood relationship carries the slightest weight with

England, and that she would refrain from attack because we have never yet crossed swords with each other. Why should England have ever had the idea of fighting us, as long as we had not the audacity to build a fleet in order to shield our coasts and our great and increasing trade? It was that—just that—which completely altered our relations. If, therefore, Great Britain has reasons for not proceeding rashly and is carefully restraining herself, we must nevertheless not conceal from ourselves that she will seize every favourable opportunity of attacking us unawares and delivering her declaration of war with the first shells at our coast resorts. Even if she is in favour of peace her allies will presumably not be inclined to perpetually burden themselves for nothing with an armament which cannot be long supported, especially by France. If she thinks the proper moment has arrived, England will not hang back.

II

RUSSIA

OUR eastern neighbour has really no cause
for a grudge against Germany. Although the
latter's conduct at the Berlin Congress of
1878 has always been regarded in Russia as
disloyal and has given rise to bad feeling, we
on our part are fully justified in recalling
past events which Prince Bismarck set out
in his *Gedanken und Erinnerungen* (Thoughts
and Recollections), from which I will therefore quote at length.

On Russia demanding whether Germany
would remain neutral if the former went to
war with Austria, Bismarck being pressed
for a definite answer replied to the Ambas-
sador : " Our first requirement is to maintain

friendship between the great monarchies, which in case of revolution had more to lose than they would gain in fighting amongst themselves. If, to our chagrin, this is not possible as between Russia and Austria, then we could very well sit still and see our friends losing or winning battles against each other, but not that one of them should be so badly wounded and damaged that its position as an independent and great Power in the Councils of Europe would be endangered." (II, page 214.) On that the Russian thunder was deflected from Galicia towards the Balkans, and Russia, at the treaty of Reichstadt, bought Austria's neutrality at the cost of Bosnia and Herzegovina.

"Even after the Berlin Congress the position of Russia remained one of the most, if not the most, favourable, which she at any time possessed after the Turkish War" (II, page 106); but "Russia, contrary to all truth and sense, gave way to exasperation at the result of the Berlin Congress. This arose in

consequence of the utterances of the Russian
Press, which, at any rate with regard to
foreign matters, is so little understood by the
people, and the pressure brought to bear.
The whole influence of Gortschakow . . .
was strong enough to produce in the Press,
with Wedomosti of Moscow at its head, a
semblance of irritation at the damage which
Russia had suffered at the Berlin Congress as
a result of Germany's perfidy.   Now no
desire of Russia was expressed at the Berlin
Congress of which Germany might not have
procured acceptance, if necessary, by means
of energetic representations to England's
Prime Minister. . . . Instead of being grateful for this it seemed to answer Russia's
policy, under the guidance of . . . Prince
Gortschakow and the Moscow papers, to continue to bring about the further estrange-
ment of Russia and Germany, for which there
was not the slightest need in the interests of
either of them.   We do not envy each other
and we cannot get anything from one another

which would be of use to us." (II, page
108.)

" During the diplomatic negotiations with
regard to the execution of the decisions of the
Berlin Congress it was expected in St. Petersburg that we would as a matter of course and
without any previous understanding between
Berlin and St. Petersburg carry out every
Russian interpretation as opposed to the
Anglo-Austrian. The request which I hinted
at and finally expressed, that Russia should
confidentially but clearly communicate her
wishes to us, was evaded, and I received the
impression that Prince Gortschakow expected me, like a lady her admirer, to guess
and represent the wishes of Russia without
the latter iterating them and taking responsibility therefor. Even in cases where we
could be presumed to be fully acquainted
with Russia's interests and views, and we
desired to voluntarily give her evidence of
our friendship, so long as this was not to our
detriment, we experienced, in place of the

recognition we expected, a grumbling dis-
approval because we did not obtain what was
expected by our Russian friends. Even when
we did so we had no better success. The
whole of this proceeding showed a calculated
dishonesty not only towards ourselves but
also to the Emperor Alexander, to whom
German policy was made to appear as dis-
honourable and unreliable." (II, pages 217-
218.)

" It is well known that in consequence of
these intrigues the Emperor Alexander was
induced to write a letter in his own hand
to the Emperor William, the contents of
which were somewhat as follows : ' If Germany continues to refuse to accommodate
itself to the voice of Russia, peace
cannot be maintained between us.' " (II,
page 219.)

As long ago as 1879 it was due only to the
wisdom and amiability of our aged Emperor
that Gortschakow's coquetting with France
did not lead to war between Germany and

F

Russia. But perhaps the French did not consider the moment opportune, as may be gathered from the Russian Prince's words : " J'aurais voulu faire la guerre, mais la France a d'autres intentions." (II, page 319.)

There is no doubt that the complaints about our behaviour at the Berlin Congress were only pretexts, the want of justification for which has long been recognized by Russian diplomatists ; but they form a convenient means of agitation and for that reason are always dug up again. The political motives which jeopardized Germany's friendship lay in another direction. We shall recognize them in following Russia's exertions for expansion.

Homer Lea is our guide. From the commencement of the eighteenth century Russia began to steer her extending movements in definite directions of which the indispensable possession of sea coasts was the first consideration. However far the Empire might extend from the Dnieper to Behring Straits and from the Arctic Ocean to the north-west shore of the Caspian, this did not enable communication with the sea, as the northern coasts are ice-bound and the Caspian has no outlet. On the north-west it was necessary to acquire the Baltic Sea by pressing Sweden. On the west to wrest Little and White Russia from the Poles. On the south they directed their gaze on the Black Sea; on the south-east the Caspian and the Caucasus had to be secured, and they fixed their eyes upon the road through Turkestan to India. On the east it was a matter of acquiring hospitable stretches of coast on the Pacific.

Russia spared no sacrifice of time and men to attain these ends and did not allow herself to be deterred by any reverses, however costly, from again traversing the same road, so as by constant endeavour to achieve success. "Russia in the course of her progress troubles herself as little about her losses in war as the Russian nature about the wildernesses created by her winter. In the eighteenth century this Empire put 4,910,000 troops into the field; of these 1,380,000 survived. In the nineteenth century the total number of troops on active service came to 4,900,000 and the losses to 1,410,000, and yet at the commencement of the eighteenth century Russia's population only amounted to 12,000,000, and at the commencement of the nineteenth century to 38,000,000. . . . The courage and determination exhibited in every Russian scheme of expansion during the seventeenth century and for two hundred years prove that Russia would never voluntarily abandon them. Hitherto these Russians have never jibbed, never hesitated. Without haste, and even after a reverse ever full of hope, sober after victory, never casting a glance at the ground which their battles have heaped with corpses, and their eyes firmly fixed on that distant but definite goal on which they were first directed." (H. Lea, pages 130-31.)

We have only to follow the expansion

towards the north-west, west and south. On the west, after the destruction of the Kingdom of Poland, Russia pressed forward as far as the Pruth and across the Weichsel, in the north-west she acquired the Baltic Provinces, and squeezed Sweden out of Finland, in the south she became mistress of the whole of the Black Sea coast from the mouth of the Danube to the Caucasus. But even then her goal was not reached. The Baltic is only connected with the ocean by narrow and dangerous channels and these Straits can with no great difficulty be completely closed. The outlet from the Black Sea through the Bosphorus and Hellespont (Dardanelles), is closed to the Russian fleet by Constantinople and various treaties. In both directions Russia, it is true, has approached substantially nearer her object, but it is no longer small weak nations but Great Powers which bar her victorious path.

The Russo-Turkish wars of the last century, although conducted ostensibly for freeing the Christian Balkan States from the Turkish yoke, were really purposed to bring them under the influence and suzerainty of Tsardom and to open the road to Constantinople. This affected Austria's interests in her most sensitive part as her entire trade to the East would have been jeopardized, and is the reason for the hostility of Russia and Austria, which must develop on every occasion when the question of the Balkan States arises.

This became apparent in the last Balkan War wherein Russia played the rôle of "Spiritus rector," and only refrained from declaring war, for which she was quite ready, on Austria, because her ally, France—just as in 1879—did not consider herself sufficiently armed to successfully interfere. For behind her allies lay the German Empire, and Italy also became more firmly bound to her allies through the jeopardy of her considerably extended interests in the Mediterranean.

Russia perceives that she will never attain

her ends in the Balkans without a victorious struggle not only with Austria but also with Germany. That binds her close to France, of whose support she is secure in all events if there is any chance of the Triple Alliance winning the mastery. Therefore it is not any interests of Russia directly conflicting with those of Germany which form the ground for their recent strong feeling against us but the opposition offered out of self-preservation by our allies to Russian endeavour in the Balkans, and the strenuous fidelity of the German Empire to its alliances.

In the north-west, Russia has advanced to the Torne-elf. An interval of only 150 kilometres separates her most advanced post from the coveted ocean harbour, Narvik, in the innermost bay of the Best Fiord; and it is only a country with five and a half millions of inhabitants which blocks her way. All preparations to fall upon the latter have been gradually made for ages; a railway was built up to the frontier river with its terminus at Tornea. But being a coast railway it is easily threatened by an enemy commanding the sea. Accordingly a second railway through the seaboard of Finland was completed up to within 400 kilometres of the frontier, and a third line is contemplated in an easterly direction. Great exertions are being made to Russianize Finland and troops have been despatched to northern garrisons. In short, we cannot avoid the impression that Russia is making great preparations to hurl a mighty blow at Sweden's resistance and to hew out a path to Narvik on the Atlantic coast. But also in this respect Germany's opposition must be reckoned with. The Swedes are well aware of the danger that threatens them. With the object of quickly despatching troops to the very thinly populated and most unfavourably situated northerly province of Norbotten and victualling them there, they have built a railway to the Torne-elf, and as a point of support have equipped a ring of fortresses on the Lule-elf, Boden,

100 kilometres from the frontier river, with all the resources of the science of fortification. Thus, breaking through to the coast will not be so easy. The whole population has however been greatly excited by the threatened danger, and judging by the procession of 33,000 peasants to Stockholm, is ready and willing to offer up life and property in defence of their fatherland. At the same time many a longing glance is directed to Germany, the mighty people that springs from the same stock and whose armies would provide a powerful bulwark for the hard-pressed little kingdom. Therefore it is not out of the reckoning that the threatening Russian danger may bring about a closer union between these two sympathetic nations with which Russia will have to reckon, and that is again an intelligible reason for her ill feeling towards Germany.

Russia has to thank us for a great deal. If it had not been for the great immigration from our country the development of her culture would be much less advanced than it actually is. It is not too much to say that everything that has been done in Russia in the way of industrial establishments has been effected principally under German management, and that even as regards the chief Government appointments the most important work is in the hands of descendants of Germans, even though they be actually Russianized. Their best officers are mostly of German descent even if they have, as true Germans, devoted their services whole-heartedly to the state and have developed into the most loyal and, as distinguished from most inborn Russians, devoted Russian subjects. The Russians have never been grateful for the obligations which Germany has laid upon Russia by the introduction of intellectual qualities and cultural development. On the contrary they have betrayed jealousy, envy and hate, and have done all they can on occasion to persecute the Germans and forcibly drive them out of the country. For the Slavs, as appears not only in Russia but also to an equal extent in the Slavonic provinces of Austria-Hungary and the Balkan Peninsula, possess a deep inborn hatred of Germany. That territory offers an all too favourable soil for the germs of mistrust which France uninterruptedly endeavours to spread, and the amicable relations between the two countries which Gortschakow in his time would have entangled but for Bismarck's acute and skilful handling, terminated after the Balkan war ended so little in favour of Russia's aims.

It cannot be denied that the bad feelings subsisting between the Balkan Allies, the Bulgarians and the Servians, have given Russian statesmen much trouble although, on the other hand, the fact that there is no statesman in the Balkans of great determination and power capable of withdrawing them, like Roumania, away from Russian suzerainty, has contributed considerably to this state of affairs. Roumania has bitterly felt Russia's ingratitude for her unselfish assistance in the war of 1877 ; but Bulgaria and Servia have already suffered so much from the unreliability and infidelity of the Tsar's Empire that it is astonishing to see them always bowing to the old yoke and following the seductive voice of St. Petersburg. It is only a short time since Servia, relying on the pledged assistance of Russia, without cause sought a conflict with Austria-Hungary and endeavoured to persist in it with astonishing stubbornness until she saw that she could not expect any help from Russia. Was not Bulgaria placed in an extremely critical position in 1885 when the Tsar, on the outbreak of the Bulgaro-Servian war, recalled various Russian officers who had accepted important positions in the Bulgarian Army? Were they not again left in the lurch last year when they relied on Russia's promise to prevent Roumania entering the ring, and instead Roumania was, to a certain extent, requested to interfere in the interests of peace just as Bulgaria was being pressed on all sides by Servia, Greece, and Turkey.

Who is in a position to judge what developments will ensue from the hurly-burly in the Balkan Peninsula ; whether Bulgaria, owing to its experiences, will ally itself with Turkey, whether Roumania will join Greece, and what part Servia, always a time server, will play ? Two things my be reckoned on : a sanguinary and, owing to the second Balkan war, much inflamed hatred by Bulgaria against Servia and Greece and—Russia's not easily discouraged anxiety to again try the political game in the Balkans which came to such a sudden end on the dissolution of the Balkan League established under her ægis. The deliberations of leading statesmen in the Balkan States, who happened "by chance" to meet in the Russian capital, could have had no other object than to forward Russian influence in order to oppose Austria's interests, and to arouse in the Balkans against Germany's ally an enemy who would

fasten on her heels as soon as she endeavoured
to defend herself against the Russian on-
slaught, or hasten to the assistance of her
ally.

It must be acknowledged that Russia's
exertions to expand meet with ever-increas-
ing and more insurmountable obstacles the
more they conflict with the interests of
European Powers, and that in face of this
opposition Russia herself requires to con-
solidate her resources, as a counterbalance.
Everyone believed that the progress of
internal development of the land and state
would be delayed by the heavy blows which
the Russian Empire sustained in East Asia,
and the consequent unrest and demoraliza-
tion amongst her officers and bureaucracy,
and finally through bad harvests. The
greater must be the surprise at Russia's
progress in every direction during recent
years. In the first place an agricultural
organization has been established which will
perhaps at last terminate the unhappy state

of the peasants. We are told that towards
the end of 1912 over a million independent
societies were formed by means of which
the peasant proprietors were enabled to free
themselves entirely. Next, the settlement of
Siberia was so energetically undertaken that
from 1907 to 1912 no less than 2,400,000
persons of both sexes were settled in Siberia,
and it is hoped that within a few years the
whole of the arable land will be brought
under the plough. The settlement of Siberia
is of enormous military importance, as in this
way it will be possible to base the defence of
East Asia on the land's own strength, and it
will not be necessary as heretofore to send
large bodies of troops from the west of the
Empire if Russia is involved in a war with
Japan or China. They are already in a
position to reinforce the present seven standing army corps in Siberia with a reserve of at
least 285,000 men formed of the inhabitants
themselves. In the same way as the development of their agriculture enabled them to

double their production between 1895 and
1911 (1,365,000,000 roubles), and the demand for agricultural machinery increased
to the amount of 119,000,000 roubles, industrial progress showed the same surprising
advance; and in spite of the constantly
increasing number the establishments do not
yet satisfy the wants of the population. The
financial conditions of the State have taken
a remarkably favourable turn since the
paper currency was withdrawn (after the
War of 1877-78) and a gold currency was
established, in addition to which the Imperial
Bank has been reorganized. They even succeeded during the Japanese War, in spite of the
tremendous war expenditure (3,600,000,000
marks—£180,000,000), in so preserving the
Bank Reserve that in October 1905 it amounted to 2,500,000,000 marks (£125,000,000).
But Russia is clever enough not to expend
this reserve on its present very considerable
outgoings for its army and defence, but
instead makes claims on its ancient banker,

France. In that way secure financial conditions will be assured for the contemplated war.

It is true that the otherwise loquacious Russian Press is silent on the subject that complete preparations on the highest scale are being made for such a war—and this is a most suspicious sign—but from what reaches our ears on the subject we ought to pay the greatest attention to them.

In all Russia's former wars want of a well developed net-work of routes—formerly of marching roads and in the last century of railways—has been a hindrance to the rapid mobilization and equipment of her armies. The greater the distances of the troop stations from each other and from the theatre of war in their extraordinarily extended Empire, the more serious was this circumstance in a country which is still to a large extent covered by considerable areas of swamp and forest. For that reason the accelerated construction of the Siberian Railway had to

G

precede the conflict with Japan, which necessarily followed the occupation of Manchuria, and even during the war the very difficult section round the shores of Lake Baikal had to be completed. Consequently a large portion of the loan of two milliard marks from France must be employed to rapidly complete the net-work of railways, so that the interior of the Empire may be linked with the German and Austro-Hungarian boundary.

But the completion of these lines of communication will take years, and therefore they will have to deal with the pressure of the allies in another manner. There are two means open; the contraction of the distance to be covered by the troops, that is to say, to the western boundary, and such an increase in the peace strength of their army that it will not be necessary to complete it by the transport by rail of an abnormal quantity of reserves. Russia has adopted both these means. Army corps have been advanced towards the frontier in three directions; towards the east against Japan and China where they have at one stroke been increased from five to seven, towards the south-east to the Caucasus against Turkey, towards the west against the German and Austro-Hungarian frontier. On the latter two new corps have been formed, and no less than nineteen new cavalry regiments.

In order to comply with the demand of France that they should not limit themselves to the defensive but should immediately commence with an advance, it was considered advisable to increase the corps to be employed in the first line to such a peace-footing that the offensive can immediately be assumed without waiting for the inclusion of any reserves. This is provided for by the extension of the period of service. This was formerly fixed at three years, namely, from the 1st/14th January to the end of the third year of service. Nevertheless, recruits were always embodied in the previous autumn and the Minister of War used, in accordance with his privilege, to permit discharges in November of the third year of service. He had also the power under the highest authority to retain the reserves with the colours even after the period of service had been completed if there were sufficient reason therefor. This right, which was exercised during the strained relations with Austria last year, has now been abandoned, as the period of service is prolonged till the 1st/14th April of what is now the fourth year of service.

What will be the result? During the period of training recruits there will be three full annual drafts of trained troops with the colours in the infantry and four in the cavalry, and the units will during this period, which is the most difficult and critical for every army, be a full quarter stronger and just as efficient as after completion of the period of training. The difference, as regards our army, which during the period of training has only one complete annual draft with the colours, can be seen at a glance. But we must take into further consideration that in case of an outbreak of war in the spring, instead of discharging the reserves they would be able to keep them back so as to have at their disposal forces almost on a war footing. Even if the Russian measures do not go as far as the transformation of the French organization, yet the latter's wishes are being taken into full account. The peace footing of the Russian Army is now judged to be as follows :—

		Of which there are in Europe	
Winter, 1913-4	1,840,000	1,322,000	troops
Summer, 1914	1,415,000	1,017,000	,,
Winter, 1914-5	1,860,000	1,337,000	,,
Summer, 1915	1,435,000	1,032,000	,,
Winter, 1915-6	1,900,000	1,047,000	,,

These figures provide approximately the full strength on a war footing during the winter months. Assuming that Russia should in general conform to the plans suggested by the French General, Cherfils, then there will be concentrated on our eastern frontier and primarily against the Provinces of East and West Prussia, fourteen or fifteen army corps of the armies of Warsaw, Wilna, St. Petersburg, and Kiev, of which eight are stationed only 80 to 200 kilometres from the frontier.

But Russia has not only prepared herself for an offensive war by the above-mentioned increase and readiness of her army, but she has also paid increased attention to the protection of her country by the extension of her fortifications. A representative of the Ministry of War declared as long ago as last June that in 1912 not only had the then fortresses been improved and extended, but also new ones were being built. The Russians are linking their system of defences on their western boundary in a northerly centre which is defended by the fortress of Kowno and the fortified Niemen-line, in a southern centre towards Galicia with the fortresses of Dubno,

Luzk and Rowno, and an advanced position the centre of which is formed by the triangular fortress chain of Warsaw—Nowo and Georgiewsk-Zegrze, the left wing of which is formed by Iwangorod and Brest Litowsk. The whole circle of these fortifications is to be energetically carried out, the Warsaw centre is to be transformed, Brest Litowsk is to be made a first-class fortress, and the Narew-Niemen line is to be made into an impregnable obstacle by means of strong defensive positions in the manner of the barrier-chains on the French eastern frontier. Great exertions are being made to make the defences of St. Petersburg even stronger than those of Kronstadt against an attack from the sea by strengthening against maritime expeditions the south and north shores of the mouth of the Bay of Finland with new fortresses—Reval-Dagō-Oesel and Sweaborg-Porkale.

If we further take into consideration the amounts set aside for the annual training of the reserves and landwehr, which rose from 2,90,000 (sic) roubles in the year 1907 to 11,165,000 roubles in the year 1913, the immense quantities of grain, arms, transport, waggons, and other war equipment which have been massed and gathered together in the frontier districts, that Russia is exerting herself to develop the greatest possible number of trained men and officers in the art of flying and the handling of airships, we cannot help believing that Russia is thinking of complying with the pressure of her ally and banker because the time for a joint operation against Germany and Austria-Hungary is favourable.

But they have not neglected to employ another means of weakening Germany's ally in the frontier districts in question by despatching agents to encourage emigration, so that tens of thousands of those liable to service leave their country and deprive the Austrian Army of irreparable strength. But the best indications of the exertions made by any country in its defence were afforded by the official statistics of the yearly estimates, and Russia's increase in respect of those for the army alone amounted in the years 1909-14 to 750,000,000 marks (£37,500,000). That is about 72 per cent., and as against 1913 they rose in 1914 by 546,000,000 (£27,300,000), *i.e.*, 43½ per cent. When we look at the navy the same thing is seen : as regards new ships for the Baltic Fleet four battleships of 23,370 tons each are ready and four in course of construction ; six armoured cruisers of 32,500 tons each are completed and four under construction ; four protected cruisers are ready and six under construction ; fifty-eight torpedo boats are completed and thirty-six under construction ; and there are thirteen submarines built and being built. These great efforts to provide a new Baltic Fleet necessitated an increase in the estimates of 302,000,000 marks between 1909 and 1913, *i.e.*, 154 per cent.

During the same period the estimates for

the French Navy rose 50 per cent., of England 29.6 per cent., but of Germany only 13.8 per cent. How unjustified therefore are the reproaches which Great Britain is perpetually casting at Germany, and only Germany, that she is immoderately increasing her navy. Why does she not do the same to her Allies—France and Russia?

III

FRANCE

IT is remarkable that Homer Lea, in his work *The Day of the Saxon*, makes absolutely no mention of France. That is rather humiliating for the latter, as it excludes France from any competition with the British Empire. She has lost all importance on the sea as regards England since the latter succeeded in the eighteenth century in beating her navy and wresting from her her considerable colonial possessions which were just beginning to flourish. The fact that France has, in the meantime, acquired considerable new possessions in other parts of the globe does not seem to trouble her former enemy, Great

Britain, as the latter has been able to retain a certain superiority. It was under this pressure that France had to give up her rights in Egypt and her designs on a colonial empire right across Africa from Senegambia to the Red Sea (Abyssinia) at the very moment when she thought she had effected the connection with her Eastern possessions by means of Fashoda. This was the only case in which her efforts to expand came into conflict with the British Empire, and the latter lost no time in putting a spoke in her wheel with brutal emphasis.

Although this treatment by the Island Empire in 1898 was deeply resented by France as a national outrage, the impression very rapidly disappeared and was lost to view behind the desire of revenge against Germany, which has prevailed since 1871, on England stepping forward to help her in the Morocco question. What is the reason for this hatred of the German Empire based on revenge, which causes all other matters in France to be relegated to the background whenever there is a demand for its settlement. The French pretend to attribute it to the ancient contest between the Gauls and the Germans about the everlasting bank of the Rhine. In order to justify the robbery of Alsace and Lorraine from Germany by Louis XIV they have put their own interpretation on history and have so stubbornly stuck to it in the schools that not only the French but also the inhabitants of the Reichsland, who derive their instruction from them, are completely permeated with this idea : *i.e.*, since the partition of the Empire of Charlemagne—who is treated by them as a French monarch—the Reichsland has been a shuttlecock between the princes and the nations so that it could never rest in peace and fully develop until King Louis XIV took pity on it and incorporated it in his Empire, when it was enabled to enjoy peace and the blessings of civilization. Even if this were so, and it is quite contrary

to all historical facts, it could not be denied
that the population of the Reichsland was
and still is to-day entirely German and not
Gallic.   In addition, the Alsatians and
Lorrainers have never been acknowledged as
entitled to full equal rights in France.   On
the contrary, they have ever been treated as
subjects of foreign origin, and have been
held up to ridicule and contempt.

But the defeats of 1870-71, which terminated in the reunion of the Reichsland, deeply
wounded the French nation in its tenderest
spot, its vanity.   That is the root of her
indelible hatred.   She could get over the
destruction of her navy by England, and the
loss of her colonies, as she still retained her
superiority on land, which was created by
Louis XIV and raised by Napoleon I to the
utmost possible limits on the Continent;
from that date the "Grande Nation" considered herself as the imparter of culture, the
ruling power in Europe.   When her boastful
arrogance under Napoleon III was met by

the unexpected resistance of Germany and the latter country (formerly despised for her division into little states and dismemberment, and jeered at for her want of civilization and culture) rose in determined unity and unexpected might and capacity not only on the battle-field but also in industry and commerce, in art and science, and herself took the lead, then the French nation, discovered in its weakness and ousted from the throne of its presumptuous might, was deeply hurt in its vanity. *Hinc illæ lacrimæ.*

The fighting powers of the inhabitants of the Reichsland are of some importance in view of the fanatical wish to win it back, as they are the descendants of old German races distinguished for their courage, who have always preserved warlike inclinations and virtues. They have furnished the French Army with many of its best soldiers and most celebrated generals. The approximately two million people of the Reichsland are of importance having regard to the decrease in the population of France, and would be of substantial assistance as regards the deficiency in officers in particular, if entry to the French Army were again open to the inhabitants of the Reichsland.

In spite of a noticeable temporary cessation of the hostile spirit (which does not prevail all over France and to an equal degree amongst the whole population), the French Government, whatever views it may have held, has always persisted in completing and perfecting her army and fortifications. That is to be attributed to two reasons : sufficient protection of the open frontier left after the loss of the Rhine frontier, and the endeavour to keep her own active force on an equal footing with the German Army. A chain of four strong ring fortresses was built on the 250 kilometres of the German frontier on the Meuse and the Moselle, of which the two barrier chains of Verdun-Toul and Epinal-Belfort serve as defensive positions on the wings and flank the gaps of Verdun-Longwy

(50 kilometres wide) and Toul-Epinal (70 kilometres). Primarily designed to support the advance of the French Army against the much more rapidly mobilizable German Army, these fortresses, now that the French hope to mobilize quicker than we do, constitute a great stronghold in a war commencing by an offensive movement. The position of Verdun-Toul in particular is extremely favourable for a defending army in consequence of its situation on the edge of the Cote de Meuse, from which steep declivities descend to the opposite plain, and this would certainly have to be penetrated by us. When Italy joined the German-Austrian League the Alpine frontier had to be more strongly protected against the former; and therefore an abnormally strong fortress consisting of Pass-barriers and strong defensive positions was erected in this neighbourhood which not only defends all the roads over the mountains but also numerous by-roads. Finally they had to obviate the possibility of an invasion of

German troops in violation of Belgium's neutrality or penetrating by way of Switzerland, so that the resisting powers of their old fortresses on these frontiers had to be improved and strengthened. Thus France has kept up a line of fortifications on the whole of her eastern frontier some 1,000 kilometres long, which should stay a surprise invasion of a hostile force. It will be quite impossible in any future war to pass these fortresses without paying them any attention as in 1870. The erection and constantly necessary repair and modernization of these fortifications could very well be carried out by means of the necessary large grants which have always been forthcoming. But the maintenance of the army on the same basis as the German Army was a more difficult matter, as this could not be attained by mere expenditure, however lavish, but only through numbers, and of that France possessed no such superfluity as she did of money. As long ago as the 'seventies she had fallen behind Germany.

With approximately the same area she had at home in 1875 only 36,900,000 against Germany's 42,700,000 inhabitants. Since then her population has only increased by 7.6 per cent. to 39,700,000, whereas Germany has reached 67,500,000, an increase therefore of 58 per cent. Consequently France could not keep pace with Germany in the annual embodiment of recruits even by constantly lowering physical requirements. She was compelled to reduce the strength of the units —in the first instance of the companies—so as to maintain the same number of battalions and afterwards also to employ men of inferior physique, substituting them for many who were engaged on indoor work, as orderlies, etc.

But owing to the small number of recruits the number of efficient soldiers who could be called up on mobilization showed a deficiency after taking into account the reserves of the German Army. If universal service had been enforced to the same extent in Germany as in France the German Army would have had

an enormous advantage in trained troops.
But the increase in size of German battalions
and consequently in the number of recruits
has not kept pace with the increase in the
population, so that the balance was not dis-
turbed to any considerable extent. This
would enable France to obtain an advantage,
at any rate temporarily, should she succeed
in bringing her standing army up to a higher
figure than is at the disposal of her eastern
neighbour. The number of trained men
capable of being added to the recruits in case
of war could of course not be increased, and
her neighbour's preponderance in effectives
could not be disputed, but the prolongation
of service with the colours from two to three
years secured an addition to the standing
army of at least 200,000 men and the further
advantage of a much more thorough training
than is possible in Germany, not only of the
men in general but also of those who aspire
to become officers of the reserve, who are
also kept for three years.

HOUR OF DESTINY

After the introduction of the three years' term of active service the French standing army reached a strength in non-commissioned officers and privates of 768,300 (inclusive of 80,000 army service corps, 24,000 gendarmes and 31,300 colonials), whereas our army had only 619,000, and even with the large increase which brought us near to universal service again, we have not yet quite overhauled the French, as we have only about 751,000 troops with the colours.

The three-year term of service was carried out in peculiar manner not without importance for the next few years. As those born in 1890 who were in the second year of service refused to remain a year longer, and voiced their sentiments by gross acts of mutiny, it was decided to discharge them in the autumn of 1913 and to embody two annual drafts of recruits at one and the same time, namely, those born in 1892 and 1893. Consequently, two annual drafts will have to be trained at the same time by means of those who have already served one year, a state of affairs which will make it almost impossible for the French Army to engage in war at the present moment. But as the commencement of service was put back a year, *i.e.*, from the year of completion of the twenty-first year to the previous one in order to legally carry out the premature embodiment of the 1893 series, those born in 1894 will have to be called up in 1914. And as those of 1891 who are now in their second year are bound for three years, it will probably be possible to keep them for 1915 also. Consequently it will be possible to have not only three but even four annual drafts in the standing army next year, *i.e.*, a greater battalion strength than is required on a war footing. Mobilization could accordingly be effected much more easily and rapidly, as not only would the various units possess their war strength, but they would be able to tell off a considerable number to form the basis of a reserve army.

France will once again in 1916 have the

opportunity of playing the same game, as the two annual drafts called out in 1913 will not be discharged till the autumn of that year. If by that time she has not attained the object of her mighty preparations, and has not succeeded in dragging Russia and England with her in an attack on Germany, she will have temporarily to forego her war of revenge if she does not want to be ruined commercially. The condition of France due to universal three years' service is nothing less than a continuous state of readiness for war. Even if a wealthy country can bear the financial sacrifice required for this state of affairs—the personal sacrifice becomes too great, having regard to the fact that not only is the peasant torn for so long a period from his plough and the artisan from his trade, but the whole youth of the country, whose scientific or technical education is of indispensable importance to the State, must have its studies interrupted for three whole years, and has got to commence again at the beginning. This youthful energy uselessly sacrificed to the idea of *revanche* would avenge itself most bitterly if it were not actually used up for the war of revenge. Therefore it follows from the military measures of France, that she will have to insist on war against Germany in the year 1915 or in any case in 1916.

But France is not content with having more than 2 per cent. (including officers) of the whole population in her standing army. She is endeavouring to get auxiliary forces from her colonies so as to be able to attain the necessary superiority in numbers without the assistance of other countries. As long ago as 1870 the "most civilized" nation drew into the ranks against us all sorts of savages from Africa, but even more can be done in this direction. In Algiers, Senegambia, and the Western Soudan especially, there is a population estimated at about thirty millions which can be of considerable assistance, and the aims of their colonial administration are primarily directed to this purpose. A German traveller who is very well acquainted with the conditions in the Soudan confirms this in the following words : " Neither commercial nor colonization schemes are sufficiently encouraged. On the contrary, their political efforts are directed to making the colony subsist on black power, black intelligence, and black money, and to produce French citizens of black blood by thousands, hundreds of thousands and millions. And, naturally, all these millions are to furnish good, enthusiastic, and patriotic French soldiers."

There are already twenty-eight battalions of so-called Senegal Guards in existence, and every year sees an increase in the planned organization. These black troops can, of course, not be transplanted to a European climate just as they are ; nevertheless the attempt to make use of them on the North Coast of Africa gave apparently good results, so that the European or Arab troops stationed there will undoubtedly be transferred to the European theatre of war and be replaced by Senegal Guards, and it may even be possible to bring over the blacks who have been acclimatized on the North Coast of Africa. In any case they will possess very considerable forces in the Soudan for the purpose of making an attack against our African colonies by the routes laid out thence and from Equatorial Africa, and attempting to take them from us, which would be well worth their while. There are already 20,000 men ready for such an enterprise. The activity with which preparations for war are being conducted in Algiers may be gathered from the constant increase of the Algerian battalions of Guards which are to be increased from five to forty-eight by annual additions, and which are already thirty-nine in number. But in addition to her African colonies France has looked for assistance elsewhere so as, notwithstanding her own want of men, to overhaul the strength of Germany's forces; Aborigines have been brought from the Antilles, it is true only to succumb in great numbers in the South of France. They were consequently shipped off to Algiers, but even there the climate did not seem to suit them. But after such attempts we should not be surprised if, during the next war, the German troops were confronted with Anna-mites and inhabitants of Madagascar and Cambodia. In the year 1912 the number of trained French troops available was stated as between $4\frac{1}{2}$ and $4\frac{3}{4}$ millions, *i.e.*, 11.3 to 12 per cent. of the whole population. As not more than 17 to 18 per cent. of males can be considered as of serviceable age, it follows that, after mobilization of such a number, only children, old men, and weaklings would be left for civil purposes. That would mean that all civil occupations would be at a standstill for the purpose of carrying on a war in such numbers. But as this is absolutely impossible in the interests of the army we had better not reckon on such an exorbitant number. Russia, with her 190,000,000 of inhabitants can submit to such a sacrifice of men, but not France.

In any case the French army, or rather the French armies if the number of army corps is doubled by the embodiment of reserves, will, even without the territorial army and its reserve, require such a large area for its operations that the Franco-German frontier would be much too short to allow it to pass through at one and the same time; thus one army will have to be employed behind the other or the outlets will have to be increased and widened. And here the question of Belgium becomes of first importance. Her sympathy with France is so well known that she can hardly be expected to offer any opposition to a march through her territory which as a neutral state it is really her duty to do. At any rate this would be a dangerous game for Belgium to play, as whatever the result might be it would probably put an end to her independence. But England also appears, as we have seen, to count on disembarking her expeditionary army at Antwerp. And they would have to join forces with the French in neutral territory—naturally under the pretext of protecting Belgium against the rapacious German Army even if the latter's troops had not yet set foot on neutral territory.

Homer Lea gives us some points with respect to neutrality which are very significant of Anglo-Saxon ideas. He thinks that the occupation of neutral territory, such as Holland and Belgium, might call forth violent opposition in England in case of a war with Germany. "That is unjustified," he says, "as the British Empire can make no impression by the sanctification of neutrality. This only forms a means of withdrawing from responsibility and imposing it on those nations who give way to the self-deception that such declarations of neutrality are inviolable. And in that respect no nation has more frequently violated neutral territory nor has any nation more often excused itself from the duty of observing neutrality than the British. . . . Should the Anglo-Saxons occupy these frontiers that will only mean territorial but not a moral violation of the neutrality of those countries. . . . Neutrality of countries under such conditions has never been and never will be a factor to be reckoned with in a war between the nations. That kind of neutrality is a modern illusion and indicates eccentric aberration." (Pages 265-66.) But I do not believe that England will exhibit the opposition assumed by Homer Lea to a violation of neutrality. I rather think that his opinions will be shared there.

France has, in the course of the last few decades, which she has undoubtedly devoted to preparing for war against Germany, had to suffer many disappointments : she has been overtaken by us in the construction of guns, and the discovery of her much vaunted smokeless powder has been a fiasco. When the Lebaudy was proudly reckoned as the sole unrivalled airship of the world, there appeared simultaneously in Germany no less than three air dirigibles all of which proved to be faster than the French one, and when the French applied themselves with great enthusiasm to the construction and development of flying machines their triumph was short-lived, as the German machines were able to show similar results within a few years. The reasons lie in the natural qualities of the French; they are intelligent, inventive, courageous and lay hold of a new idea with great skill and enthusiasm ; but they are not careful workmen, and lack the untiring patience of the Germans, who, unlike the French satisfied with a momentary success and then taking up something new, are not content with their results and are always striving to attain something better and more perfect.

But one weapon the French know how to wield with adroitness : the fostering of insurrection in our border country, the Reichsland. I must lay emphasis on the fact that in the coming war, at any rate in the first days of preparation, this is destined to play a fatal part, but will not prove a blessing to the poor inhabitants if they do not resist this unholy influence.

IV

CONCLUSIONS

THE European nations of German and Latin origin have since the downfall of the Roman Empire rightly regarded themselves as the pioneers of civilization, and have consequently considered themselves called upon to impress their stamp on the other portions of the earth which have been opened up by them, and at the same time to exercise spiritual, but to a larger extent political powers. But in the development of nations we always find that the population, to whatever extent it may have been subjected, acquires all the qualities and character by means of which the ruling nation was able to make itself master, and then endeavours to break its fetters, whether they be spiritual or political. From this arises the evident danger of the European Great Powers in that they are gradually ousted from their ruling position on the earth and are relegated to the Old World. And the more so if they have singly to meet new-born world powers. We saw the commencement of this new era during the Russo-Japanese War; as, even if Russia is not to be considered in the pre-eminence of its culture as a prominent member of the European Powers, yet, as distinguished from Japan, she represented European civilization. And in the Pacific, where she met defeat, the future battles for the dominion of the world will be decided between the European, Asiatic and American nations. The Emperor William II years ago issued the following prophetic warning : "Nations of Europe, guard your most holy treasures." What he meant by that was clearly indicated.

No one will dispute this view, and it would be sufficient reason for the European nations to unite in jointly warding off this danger. Nothing further would be necessary than a few concessions which would hurt nobody, a fair adjustment of indispensable expansion of territory, trade or power, a surrender of superfluous possessions and the suppression of all selfish efforts to take revenge on or repress a neighbour. Do the interests of each so conflict that no portion can be sacrificed to avoid the loss of the whole? If the peace conferences at The Hague would take these views into consideration in the hope of arriving at a union of the Powers in common defence, then their importance to Europe could not be sufficiently appreciated. But how different are the conditions! Divided into two large hostile camps, the six Great Powers, groaning under the grievous burden of their armaments, stand opposed, talk only of peace and friendship, and then one side is consumed with the desire to strike, whilst the other, hand on sword, has to be ever ready for the conflict in which Europe will be torn to pieces and for many years rendered incapable of meeting the danger to its commercial, political and military rule which threatens it from without.

Since King Edward of England, under the illusion that the growing land and sea power of the German Empire was a danger to the existence of the British Empire as a world power, concluded an alliance with all former enemies of Great Britain and spared no trouble to isolate us and surround us with hostile forces, Europe has been living in constant anticipation of a terrible conflict. That it has not broken out long since, and that so favourable an opportunity as the War in the Balkans did not fire the powder, and that it was just England who held back her threatening allies, is in my view principally to be attributed to the cold-blooded British commercial spirit. England would have no objection to the Continental Powers coming to blows and lacerating each other ; but then she might have to bear part of the expense. What advantage would any side derive from victory in such a war ? A devastated country and empty coffers. What country if conquered would be able to pay the war indemnity ? It is difficult to see what could be " got " out of such a war, and as Great Britain would be compelled to take part because she herself has the largest interest in the destruction of the German Navy, and could not hope to leave the battlefield without very serious losses and without any advantage, she for the moment avoids the execution of the plans drawn up by herself.

But the spirits you have called up cannot now be got rid of. France's inspired desire for vengeance against the German Empire, and the inflamed hatred of Russia against Austria-

Hungary, who bars her progress, have compelled both countries to enhance their war preparations, which can only be maintained for a short time. As a matter of fact these preparations cannot be really distinguished from actual readiness for war, and by the spring of 1915 they will have been so nearly completed that we must be prepared day by day to expect the invasion of a mighty horde such as has never been seen in Europe or on earth. And then the hour of the German Empire and its Allies will strike, then we shall have to fight harder than ever, but then also will we show to the world an enthusiasm, a resignation, and spirit of sacrifice even greater and more valiant than in the wars of liberation, for never will a nation have been attacked with greater injustice than in this coming war. Never has any nation been so patient and long-suffering under imposition and provocation from all sides as Germany has been in recent years. If ever a nation and a ruler have shown firm determination to remain the guardians of peace it is Germany and the Emperor William II.

And just as last year the Government immediately answered France's threatening measure, the reintroduction of three years' service, with a powerful addition to our forces, just as the German people submitted to the depletion of its means without demur —nay rather with a certain sense of high-minded and joyful sacrifice for the sake of the Fatherland—so we may be sure that all preparations will be duly made not only with regard to the forces but also provision for the financial and commercial side. For so prolonged a war, which will demand all the resources of the countries involved, will be carried on not only with the weapons of army and navy, but also by pitting against each other their respective commercial and financial resources. But it must not be imagined that five or six million soldiers are all of a sudden going to pour over our borders and simply crush our armies. At first there is only the regular army to be considered after deducting all troops that have to be retained in the fortresses and for various other purposes, as the embodiment and the equipment of the reserve armies requires considerable time. Secondly, large masses of troops require large operating areas, as armies only approximately similar in size can be employed in a certain space. In this respect the operating and fighting conditions of our modern armies of millions differ essentially from those of the smaller armies such as Frederick the Great and even Napoleon had at their disposal. In those days strategists were always able to follow the course of a battle from some commanding point and seize their opportunities accordingly. This was out of the question even at Metz and Sedan, as the still comparatively small masses of troops had to be extended over many miles to employ them in battle. And what an enormous extent of ground the Manchurian battles covered! So there will be no question in the coming battles of overpowering masses, of crushing by superior forces ; one man will not have to fight five or six ; the opposing lines will be equally thick or thin. And thus in the future as in the past, the moral qualities coupled with the physical fitness, activity, and gunnery of the individual soldier will decide the issue in a skirmish, and correct judgment of the enemy and his movements as well as employment of the troops at the right time and place, on the part of the commanders, will decide the battle. The French Army will derive no advantage from its excessive increase in numbers, which is beyond the strength of the country, as this effort has led to the inclusion not only of men absolutely fit for campaigning, but also of many who are weakly and unfit, and this may prove to be a heavy burden to the army. When it is seen how few French soldiers are able to withstand disease—for example, at the moment no less than 36 per cent. of those in active service are released through death,

135

disease or debility—it will be recognized that many will succumb to the exertions of heavy marches, insufficient nourishment and constant nervous excitement. It cannot be denied that the longer term of service in the French as well as in the Russian Army is capable through judicious training of ensuring more efficiency than is possible in our term of two years. But this requires in particular conscientious and willing instructors and consequently a corps of officers and N.C.O.'s of supreme excellence, which judging by the events of the Japanese war, will hardly be found in the Russian army; and in France the quality of officers and privates alike is substantially influenced by their fatal participation in politics. There is one characteristic of the German soldier which is of great advantage to our army and which is absent in the Latin races; both the reserves and the Landwehr retain what they have learned in active service with frequently surprising tenacity.

To fully appreciate the value of this quality it is necessary to see a company of the Landwehr in the field. I have myself noticed in the case of pioneers, whose technical knowledge is the most easily forgotten, that they only require one or two days' practice in order to completely recover their infantry training, and hardly require a short course of instruction in technical work before they show the same skill as if they had been discharged yesterday instead of ten years ago.

If there is to be a conflict we shall enter it with the same consciousness and conviction of victory as in 1870, mindful that numbers alone will not ensure it but that it will fall to him who can hold out longest in endurance and money. As for the rest, the motto adapted from an old saying which the architect of the Palace of Peace set over the window of the great hall, *Si vis pacem, para justitiam,* is all very well, but absolute justice does not exist. Who will decide the dispute

HOUR OF DESTINY

between Germany and France as to the right of possession of the Reichsland? Each of them will ever maintain that his title is the only good one. Therefore it is better to restore the sentence to its old form :—

Si vis pacem, para bellum !

66
74

The Secret History of the Court of Berlin

THE PRIVATE LIVES OF KAISER WILLIAM II AND HIS CONSORT

From the Papers and Diaries of a Lady-in-Waiting to the German Empress Queen

By HENRY WILLIAM FISHER

Crown 8vo, 320 pages, **1s.** net   Ninth Impression

This book, **the most intimate on a living monarch ever published,** reveals the private lives of the Emperor and his Consort, of his Ministers and Great Officials, and has been described as **'Written as no one ever dared write before.'** These astounding revelations show unmistakably that **the Kaiser's uncontrollable ambition would inevitably lead him into a scheme for setting the world on fire by a European war.**

JOHN LONG, Ltd., Publishers, LONDON